WORKERS OF ALL COUNTRIES, UNITE!

Karl Marx

KARL MARX

CRITIQUE OF THE GOTHA PROGRAMME

FOREIGN LANGUAGES PRESS
PEKING 1972

First Edition 1972

PUBLISHER'S NOTE

The present English edition of Karl Marx's *Critique of the Gotha Programme* contains Marx's "Marginal Notes to the Programme of the German Workers' Party", his letter to Wilhelm Bracke of May 5, 1875, and Engels' "Foreword", his letter to August Bebel of March 18-28, 1875, and his letter to Karl Kautsky of February 23, 1891, which have been reprinted from the English edition of *Selected Works of Karl Marx and Frederick Engels*, Vol. II, Foreign Languages Publishing House, Moscow, 1951, with corrections of the translation where necessary, and with revisions of the "Marginal Notes" according to the original German manuscript as given in the *Works of Marx and Engels*, Vol. 19. Engels' letter to Bracke of October 11, 1875, and his letter to Bebel of October 12, 1875, have been reprinted from the English edition of the *Critique* published by International Publishers, New York, 1938, likewise with corrections of the translation. Engels' other letters have been translated from the German original.

Most of the notes at the end of the book are translations of those in the Chinese edition, while the rest are from the English editions mentioned above.

Printed in the People's Republic of China

This material is filed with the Department of Justice where the registration statement of China Books & Periodicals, 2929 - 24th St., San Francisco, CA., 94110 and 125 Fifth Ave., New York, N.Y. 10003 and 900 W. Armitage Ave., Chicago, Il. 60614 as an agent of Guozi Shudian, Peking, China or Xunhasaba, Hanoi, Vietnam under the Foreign Agents Registration Act of 1938, as amended, is available for public inspection. Registration does not indicate approval of the contents of this material by the United States Government. The sole relationship of registrant to this material is that of purchaser and seller.

CONTENTS

CRITIQUE OF THE GOTHA PROGRAMME[1]

Written by Karl Marx, April — early May 1875

Published in *Die Neue Zeit*, No. 18, Vol. I, 1891, with abridgements

Original in German

FOREWORD BY FREDERICK ENGELS

The manuscript published here — the covering letter to Bracke as well as the critique of the draft programme — was sent in 1875, shortly before the Gotha Unity Congress,[2] to Bracke for communication to Geib, Auer, Bebel and Liebknecht to be subsequently returned to Marx. Since the Halle Party Congress[3] has put the discussion of the Gotha Programme on the agenda of the Party, I think I would be guilty of suppression if I any longer withheld from the public this important — perhaps the most important — document relevant to this discussion.

But the manuscript has yet another and more far-reaching significance. Here for the first time Marx's attitude to the line adopted by Lassalle in his agitation from the very beginning is clearly and firmly set forth, both as regards Lassalle's economic principles and his tactics.

The ruthless severity with which the draft programme is dissected here, the mercilessness with which the results obtained are enunciated and the shortcomings of the draft laid bare — all this today, after fifteen years, can no longer give offence. Specific Lassalleans now exist only abroad as isolated ruins, and in Halle the Gotha Programme was given up even by its creators as altogether inadequate.

Nevertheless, I have omitted a few sharp personal expressions and judgements where these were immaterial, and replaced them by dots. Marx himself would have done so if he had published the manuscript today. The violence of the language in some passages was provoked by two circumstances. In the first place, Marx and I had been more intimately connected with the German movement than with any other; we were, therefore, bound to be particularly perturbed by the decidedly retrograde step manifested by this draft programme. And secondly, we were at that time, hardly two years after the Hague Congress of the International,[4] engaged in the most violent struggle against Bakunin and his anarchists, who made us responsible for everything that happened in the labour movement in Germany; hence we had to expect that we would also be saddled with the secret paternity of this programme. These considerations do not now exist and so there is no necessity for the passages in question.

For reasons arising from the Press Law, also, a few sentences have been indicated only by dots. Where I have had to choose a milder expression this has been enclosed in square brackets. Otherwise the text has been reproduced word for word.

F. Engels

London, January 6, 1891

MARX TO WILHELM BRACKE

London, May 5, 1875

Dear Bracke,

When you have read the following critical marginal notes on the Unity Programme, would you be so good as to send them on to Geib and Auer, Bebel and Liebknecht for them to examine. I am exceedingly busy and have already overstepped the limit of work allowed me by the doctor. Hence it was anything but a "pleasure" to write such a lengthy screed. It was, however, necessary so that the steps to be taken by me later on would not be misinterpreted by our friends in the Party for whom this communication is intended.

After the Unity Congress has been held, Engels and I will publish a short declaration to the effect that our position is altogether remote from the said programme of principles and that we have nothing to do with it.

This is indispensable because the opinion — the entirely erroneous opinion — is held abroad, assiduously nurtured by enemies of the Party, that we secretly guide from here the movement of the so-called Eisenach Party. In a Russian book[5] that has recently appeared, Bakunin still makes me responsible, for example, not only for all the programmes, etc., of that party but even for every step taken by Liebknecht from the day of his co-operation with the People's Party.[6]

Apart from this, it is my duty not to give recognition, even by diplomatic silence, to what in my opinion is a thoroughly objectionable programme that demoralizes the Party.

Every step of real movement is more important than a dozen programmes. If, therefore, it was not possible — and the conditions of the time did not permit it — to go *beyond* the Eisenach programme, one should simply have concluded an agreement for action against the common enemy. But by drawing up a programme of principles (instead of postponing this until it has been prepared for by a considerable period of common activity) one sets up before the whole world landmarks by which it measures the level of the Party movement.

The Lassallean leaders came because circumstances forced them to come. If they had been told in advance that there would be no bargaining about principles, they would have *had* to be content with a programme of action or a plan of organization for common action. Instead of this, one permits them to arrive armed with mandates, recognizes these mandates on one's part as valid, and thus surrenders unconditionally to those who are themselves in need of help. To crown the whole business, they are holding a congress again *before* the *Congress of Compromise*, while one's own party is holding its congress *post festum*.[7] One obviously had a desire to stifle all criticism and to give one's own party no opportunity for reflection. One knows that the mere fact of unification is satisfying to the workers, but it is a mistake to believe that this momentary success is not bought at too high a price.

For the rest, the programme is no good at all, even apart from its sanctification of the Lassallean articles of faith.

I shall be sending you in the near future the last parts of the French edition of *Capital*. The continuation of the printing was held up for a considerable time owing to the ban of the French government. The thing will be ready this week or the beginning of next week. Have you received the previous six parts? Please let me have the address of Bernhard Becker, to whom I must also send the final parts.[8]

The bookshop of the *Volksstaat*[9] has peculiar ways. Up to this moment, for example, I have not been sent a single copy of the publication on the Cologne Communist Trial.[10]

With best wishes,

Yours,

Karl Marx

MARGINAL NOTES
TO THE PROGRAMME
OF THE GERMAN WORKERS' PARTY

I

1. "Labour is the source of all wealth and all culture, *and since* useful labour is possible only in society and through society, the proceeds of labour belong undiminished with equal right to all members of society."

First Part of the Paragraph: "Labour is the source of all wealth and all culture."

Labour is *not the source* of all wealth. *Nature* is just as much the source of use values (and it is surely of such that material wealth consists!) as labour, which itself is only the manifestation of a force of nature, human labour power. The above phrase is to be found in all children's primers and is correct in so far as it is *implied* that labour is performed with the appurtenant subjects and instruments. But a socialist programme cannot allow such bourgeois phrases to pass over in silence the *conditions* that alone give them meaning. Only in so far as man from the beginning behaves towards nature, the primary source of all instruments and subjects of labour, as an owner, treats her as belonging to him, does his labour become the source of use values, therefore also of wealth. The bourgeois have very good grounds for falsely ascribing *supernatural creative power* to labour; since precisely from the fact that labour depends on nature it follows that the man who possesses no other property than his labour power must, in all conditions of society and culture, be the slave of other men who have made themselves the owners of the objective conditions of labour. He can work only with their permission, hence live only with their permission.

Let us now leave the sentence as it stands, or rather limps. What would one have expected in conclusion? Obviously this:

"Since labour is the source of all wealth, no one in society can appropriate wealth except as the product of labour. Therefore, if he himself does not work, he lives by the labour of others and also acquires his culture at the expense of the labour of others."

Instead of this, by means of the verbal rivet "*and since*" a second proposition is added in order to draw a conclusion from it and not from the first one.

Second Part of the Paragraph: "Useful labour is possible only in society and through society."

According to the first proposition, labour was the source of all wealth and all culture; therefore no society is possible without labour. Now we learn, conversely, that no "useful" labour is possible without society.

One could just as well have said that only in society can useless and even socially harmful labour become a branch of gainful occupation, that only in society can one live by being idle, etc., etc. — in short, one could just as well have copied the whole of Rousseau.

And what is "useful" labour? Surely only labour which produces the intended useful result. A savage — and man was a savage after he had ceased to be an ape — who kills an animal with a stone, who collects fruits, etc., performs "useful" labour.

Thirdly. The Conclusion: "And since useful labour is possible only in society and through society, the proceeds of labour belong undiminished with equal right to all members of society."

A fine conclusion! If useful labour is possible only in society and through society, the proceeds of labour belong to society — and only so much therefrom accrues to the individual worker as is not required to maintain the "condition" of labour, society.

In fact, this proposition has at all times been made use of by the champions of the *prevailing state of society.* First come the claims of the government and everything that clings to it, since it is the social organ for the maintenance of the social order; then come the claims of the various kinds of owners of private property, since the various kinds of private property are the foundations of society, etc. One sees that such hollow phrases can be twisted and turned as desired.

The first and second parts of the paragraph have some intelligible connection only in the following wording:

"Labour becomes the source of wealth and culture only as social labour," or, what is the same thing, "in and through society."

This proposition is incontestably correct, for although isolated labour (its material conditions presupposed) can also create use values, it can create neither wealth nor culture.

But equally incontestable is this other proposition:

"In proportion as labour develops socially, and becomes thereby a source of wealth and culture, poverty and destitution develop among the workers, and wealth and culture among the non-workers."

This is the law of all history hitherto. What, therefore, had to be done here, instead of setting down general phrases about "labour" and "society," was to prove concretely how in present capitalist society the material, etc., conditions have at last been created which enable and compel the workers to lift this historical curse.

In fact, however, the whole paragraph, bungled in style and content, is only there in order to inscribe the Lassallean catchword of the "undiminished proceeds of labour" as a slogan at the top of the Party banner. I shall return later to the "proceeds of labour," "equal right," etc., since the same thing recurs in a somewhat different form.

> 2. "In present-day society, the instruments of labour are the monopoly of the capitalist class; the resulting dependence of the working class is the cause of misery and servitude in all its forms."

This sentence, borrowed from the Rules of the International, is incorrect in this "improved" edition.

In present-day society the instruments of labour are the monopoly of the landowners (the monopoly of property in land is even the basis of the monopoly of capital) *and* the capitalists. In the passage in question, the Rules of the International do not mention either the one or the other class of monopolists. They speak of the "*monopoly of the means of labour, that is, the sources of life.*" The addition, "*sources of life,*" makes it sufficiently clear that land is included in the instruments of labour.

The correction was introduced because Lassalle, for reasons now generally known, attacked *only* the capitalist class and not the landowners. In England, the capitalist is usually not even the owner of the land on which his factory stands.

> 3. "The emancipation of labour demands the promotion of the instruments of labour to the common property of society and the co-operative regulation of the total labour with a fair distribution of the proceeds of labour."

"Promotion of the instruments of labour to the common property"! Obviously this ought to read their "conversion into the common property"; but this only in passing.

What are "proceeds of labour"? The product of labour or its value? And in the latter case, is it the total value of the product or only that part of the value which labour has newly added to the value of the means of production consumed?

"Proceeds of labour" is a loose notion which Lassalle has put in the place of definite economic conceptions.

What is "a fair distribution"?

Do not the bourgeois assert that the present-day distribution is "fair"? And is it not, in fact, the only "fair" distribution on the basis of the present-day mode of production? Are economic relations regulated by legal conceptions, or do not, on the contrary, legal relations arise from economic ones? Have not also the socialist sectarians the most varied notions about "fair" distribution?

To understand what is implied in this connection by the phrase "fair distribution," we must take the first paragraph and this one together. The latter presupposes a society wherein "the instruments of labour are common property and the total labour is co-operatively regulated," and from the first paragraph we learn that "the proceeds of labour belong undiminished with equal right to all members of society."

"To all members of society"? To those who do not work as well? What remains then of the "undiminished proceeds of labour"? Only to those members of society who work? What remains then of the "equal right" of all members of society?

But "all members of society" and "equal right" are obviously mere phrases. The kernel consists in this, that in this communist society every worker must receive the "undiminished" Lassallean "proceeds of labour."

Let us take first of all the words "proceeds of labour" in the sense of the product of labour; then the co-operative proceeds of labour are the *total social product*.

From this must now be deducted:

First, cover for replacement of the means of production used up.

Secondly, additional portion for expansion of production.

Thirdly, reserve or insurance funds against accidents, dislocations caused by natural calamities, etc.

These deductions from the "undiminished proceeds of labour" are an economic necessity and their magnitude is to be determined according to available means and forces, and partly by computation of probabilities, but they are in no way calculable by equity.

There remains the other part of the total product, intended to serve as means of consumption.

Before this is divided among individuals, there has to be deducted again, from it:

First, the general costs of administration not directly belonging to production.

This part will, from the outset, be very considerably restricted in comparison with present-day society and it diminishes in proportion as the new society develops.

Secondly, that which is intended for the common satisfaction of needs, such as schools, health services, etc.

From the outset this part grows considerably in comparison with present-day society and it grows in proportion as the new society develops.

Thirdly, funds for those unable to work, etc., in short, for what is included under so-called official poor relief today.

Only now do we come to the "distribution" which the programme, under Lassallean influence, alone has in view in its narrow fashion, namely, to that part of the means of consumption which is divided among the individual producers of the co-operative society.

The "undiminished proceeds of labour" have already surreptitiously become converted into the "diminished" proceeds, although what is withheld from the producer in his capacity as a private individual benefits him directly or indirectly in his capacity as a member of society.

Just as the phrase of the "undiminished proceeds of labour" has disappeared, so now does the phrase "the proceeds of labour" disappear altogether.

Within the co-operative society based on common ownership of the means of production, the producers do not exchange their products; just as little does the labour employed on the products appear here *as the value* of these products, as an objective quality possessed by them, since now, in contrast to capitalist society, individual labour no longer exists in an indirect fashion but directly as a component part of the total labour. The phrase "proceeds of labour," objectionable also today on account of its ambiguity, thus loses all meaning.

What we have to deal with here is a communist society, not as it has *developed* on its own foundations, but, on the contrary, just as it *emerges* from capitalist society; which is thus in every respect, economically, morally and intellectually, still stamped with the birth marks of the old society from whose womb it emerges. Accordingly, the individual producer receives back from society — after the deductions have been made — exactly what he gives to it. What he has given to it is his individual quantum of labour. For example, the social working day consists of the sum of the individual hours of work; the individual labour time of the individual producer is the part of the social working day contributed by him, his share in it. He receives a certificate from society that he has furnished such and such an amount of labour (after deducting his labour for the common funds), and with this certificate he draws from the social stock of means of consumption as much as the same amount of labour costs. The same amount of labour which he has given to society in one form he receives back in another.

Here obviously the same principle prevails as that which regulates the exchange of commodities, as far as this is exchange of equal values. Content and form are changed, because under the altered circumstances no one can give anything except his labour, and because, on the other hand, nothing can pass into the ownership of individuals except individual means of consumption. But, as far as the distribution of the latter among the individual producers is concerned, the same principle prevails as in the exchange of commodity-equivalents: a given amount of labour in one form is exchanged for an equal amount of labour in another form.

Hence, *equal right* here is still — in principle — *bourgeois right,* although principle and practice are no longer at loggerheads, while the exchange of equivalents in commodity exchange exists only *on the average* and not in the individual case.

In spite of this advance, this *equal right* is still perpetually burdened with a bourgeois limitation. The right of the producers is *proportional* to the labour they supply; the equality consists in the fact that measurement is made with an *equal standard,* labour. But one man is superior to another physically or mentally and so supplies more labour in the same time, or can work for a longer time; and labour, to serve as a measure, must be defined by its duration or intensity, otherwise it ceases to be a standard of measurement. This *equal* right is an unequal right for unequal labour. It recognizes no class differences, because everyone is only a worker like everyone else; but it tacitly recognizes unequal individual endowment and thus productive capacity of the worker as natural privileges. *It is, therefore, a right of inequality, in its content, like every right.* Right by its very nature can consist only in the application of an equal standard; but unequal individuals (and they would not be different individuals if they were not unequal) are measurable only by the same standard in so far as they are brought under the same point of view, are taken from one *definite* side only, for instance, in the present case, are regarded *only as workers,* and nothing more is seen in them, everything else being ignored. Further, one worker is married, another not; one has more children than another, and so on and so forth. Thus, with an equal performance of labour, and hence an equal share in the social consumption fund, one will in fact receive more than another, one will be richer than another, and so on. To avoid all these defects, right instead of being equal would have to be unequal.

But these defects are inevitable in the first phase of communist society as it is when it has just emerged after prolonged birth pangs from capitalist society. Right can never be higher than the economic structure of society and its cultural development conditioned thereby.

In a higher phase of communist society, after the enslaving subordination of the individual to the division of labour, and with it also the antithesis between mental and physical labour, has vanished; after labour has become not only a means of life but itself life's prime want; after the productive forces have also increased with the all-round development of the individual, and all the springs of co-operative wealth flow more abundantly — only then can the narrow horizon of bourgeois right be crossed in its entirety and society inscribe on its banners: From each according to his ability, to each according to his needs!

I have dealt more at length with the "undiminished proceeds of labour," on the one hand, and with "equal right" and "fair distribution," on the other, in order to show what a serious crime it is to attempt, on the one hand, to force on our Party again, as dogmas, ideas which in a certain period had some meaning but have now become obsolete verbal rubbish, while again perverting, on the other, the realistic outlook, which it cost so much effort to instil into the Party but which has taken root in it, by means of ideological nonsense about right, etc., so common among the democrats and French Socialists.

Quite apart from the analysis so far, it was in general a mistake to make a fuss about so-called *distribution* and put the principal stress on it.

The prevailing distribution of the means of consumption is only a consequence of the distribution of the conditions of production themselves; the latter distribution, however, is a feature of the mode of production itself. The capitalist mode of production, for example, rests on the fact that the material conditions of production are in the hands of non-workers in the form of property in capital and land, while the masses are only owners of the personal condition of production, of labour power. If the elements of production are so distributed, then the present-day distribution of the means of consumption results automatically. If the material conditions of production are the co-operative property of the workers themselves, then there likewise results a distribution of the means of consumption different from the present one. Vulgar socialism (and from it in turn a section of the democracy) has taken over from the bourgeois economists the consideration and treatment of distribution as independent of the mode of production and hence the presentation of socialism as turning principally on distribution. After the real relation has long been made clear, why retrogress again?

> 4. "The emancipation of labour must be the work of the working class, relatively to which all other classes are *only one reactionary mass.*"

The first strophe is taken from the introductory words of the Rules of the International, but "improved." There it is said: "The emancipation of the working class must be the act of the workers themselves"; here, on the contrary, the "working class" has to emancipate — what? "Labour." Let him understand who can.

In compensation, the antistrophe, on the other hand, is a Lassallean quotation of the first water: "relatively to which (the working class) all other classes are *only one reactionary mass.*"

In the *Communist Manifesto* it is said: "Of all the classes that stand face to face with the bourgeoisie today, the proletariat alone is a *really revolutionary class.* The other classes decay and finally disappear in the face of modern industry; the proletariat is its special and essential product."[11]

The bourgeoisie is here conceived as a revolutionary class — as the bearer of large-scale industry — relatively to the feudal lords and the lower middle class, who desire to maintain all social positions that are the creation of obsolete modes of production. Thus they do not form *together with the bourgeoisie* only one reactionary mass.

On the other hand, the proletariat is revolutionary relatively to the bourgeoisie because, having itself grown up on the basis of large-scale industry, it strives to strip off from production the capitalist character that the bourgeoisie seeks to perpetuate. But the *Manifesto* adds that the "lower middle class" . . . is becoming revolutionary "in view of [its] impending transfer into the proletariat."

From this point of view, therefore, it is again nonsense to say that it, together with the bourgeoisie, and with the feudal lords into the bargain, "forms only one reactionary mass" relatively to the working class.

Has one proclaimed to the artisans, small manufacturers, etc., and *peasants* during the last elections:[12] Relatively to us you, together with the bourgeoisie and feudal lords, form only one reactionary mass?

Lassalle knew the *Communist Manifesto* by heart, as his faithful followers know the gospels written by him. If, therefore, he falsified it so grossly, this occurred only to put a good colour on his alliance with absolutist and feudal opponents against the bourgeoisie.

In the above paragraph, moreover, his oracular saying is dragged in by main force without any connection with the botched quotation from the Rules of the International. Thus it is here simply an impertinence, and indeed not at all displeasing to Herr Bismarck, one of those cheap pieces of insolence in which the Marat of Berlin[13] deals.

> 5. "The working class strives for its emancipation first of all *within the framework of the present-day national state,* conscious that the necessary result of its efforts, which are common to the workers of all civilized countries, will be the international brotherhood of peoples."

Lassalle, in opposition to the *Communist Manifesto* and to all earlier socialism, conceived the workers' movement from the narrowest national standpoint. He is being followed in this — and that after the work of the International!

It is altogether self-evident that, to be able to fight at all, the working class must organize itself at home *as a class* and that its own country is the immediate arena of its struggle. In so far its class struggle is national, not in substance, but, as the *Communist Manifesto* says, "in form." But the "framework of the present-day national state," for instance, the German Empire, is itself in its turn economically "within the framework" of the world market, politically "within the framework" of the system of states. Every businessman knows that German trade is at the same time foreign trade, and the greatness of Herr Bismarck consists, to be sure, precisely in his kind of *international* policy.

And to what does the German workers' party reduce its internationalism? To the consciousness that the result of its efforts will be "*the international brotherhood of peoples*" — a phrase borrowed from the bourgeois League of Peace and Freedom,[14] which is intended to pass as equivalent to the international brotherhood of the working classes in the joint struggle against the ruling classes and their governments. Not a word, therefore, *about the international functions* of the German working class! And it is thus that it is to challenge its own bourgeoisie — which is already linked up in brotherhood against it with the bourgeois of all other countries — and Herr Bismarck's international policy of conspiracy![15]

In fact, the internationalist avowal of the programme stands *infinitely below even* that of the Free Trade Party. The latter also asserts that the result of its efforts will be "the international brotherhood of peoples." But it also *does* something to make trade international and by no means contents itself with the consciousness — that all peoples are carrying on trade at home.

The international activity of the working class does not in any way depend on the existence of the *International Working Men's Association.* This was only the first attempt to create a central organ for that activity, an attempt which was a lasting success on account of the impulse it gave but which was no longer realizable in its *first historical form* after the fall of the Paris Commune.

Bismarck's *Norddeutsche* was absolutely right when it announced, to the satisfaction of its master, that the German workers' party had sworn off internationalism in the new programme.[16]

II

> "Starting from these basic principles, the German workers' party strives by all legal means for the *free state — and —* socialist society: the abolition of the wage system *together with* the *iron law of wages* — and — exploitation in every form; the elimination of all social and political inequality."

I shall return to the "free" state later.

So, in future, the German workers' party has got to believe in Lassalle's "iron law of wages"![17] That this may not be lost, the nonsense is perpetrated of speaking of the "abolition of the wage system" (it should read: system of wage labour) "*together with* the iron law of wages." If I abolish wage labour, then naturally I abolish its laws also, whether they are of "iron" or sponge. But Lassalle's attack on wage labour turns almost solely on this so-called law. In order, therefore, to prove that Lassalle's sect has conquered, the "wage system" must be abolished "*together with* the iron law of wages" and not without it.

It is well known that nothing of the "iron law of wages" is Lassalle's except the word "iron" borrowed from Goethe's "great, eternal iron laws."[18] The word *iron* is a label by which the true believers recognize one another. But if I take the law with Lassalle's stamp on it and, consequently, in his sense, then I must also take it with his substantiation for it. And what is that? As Lange already showed, shortly after Lassalle's death, it is the Malthusian theory of population (preached by Lange himself).[19] But if this theory is correct, then again I *cannot* abolish the law even if I abolish wage labour a hundred times over, because the law then governs not only the system of wage labour but *every* social system. Basing themselves directly on this, the economists have been proving for fifty years and more that socialism cannot abolish poverty, *which has its basis in nature*, but can only make it *general*, can only distribute it simultaneously over the whole surface of society!

But all this is not the main thing. *Quite apart* from the *false* Lassallean formulation of the law, the truly outrageous step backwards consists in the following:

Since Lassalle's death the path has been broken in *our* Party for the scientific understanding that wages are not what they *appear* to be, namely, the *value*, or *price, of labour*, but only a masked form for the *value*, or *price, of labour power*. Thereby the whole previous bourgeois conception of wages, as well as all the previous criticism directed against this conception, was thrown overboard once for all and it was made clear that the wage worker has permission to work for his own subsistence, that is, *to live*, only in so far as he works for a certain time gratis for the capitalist (and hence also for the latter's co-consumers of surplus value); that the whole capitalist system of production turns on the increase of this gratis labour by extending the working day or by developing the productivity, increasing the intensity of labour power, etc.; that, consequently, the system of wage labour is a system of slavery, and indeed of a slavery which becomes more severe in proportion as the social productive forces of labour develop, whether the worker receives better or worse payment. And after this understanding has gained more and more ground in our Party, one returns to Lassalle's dogmas, although one must have known that Lassalle *did not know* what wages were, but following in the wake of the bourgeois economists took the appearance for the essence of the matter.

It is as if, among slaves who have at last got behind the secret of slavery and broken out in rebellion, a slave still in thrall to obsolete notions were to inscribe on the programme of the rebellion: Slavery must be abolished because the feeding of slaves in the system of slavery cannot exceed a certain low maximum!

Does not the mere fact that the representatives of our Party were capable of perpetrating such a monstrous attack on the widespread understanding among the mass of our Party prove by itself with what criminal levity and with what lack of conscience they set to work in drawing up this compromise programme!

Instead of the indefinite concluding phrase of the paragraph, "the elimination of all social and political inequality," it ought to have been said that with the abolition of class distinctions all social and political inequality arising from them would disappear of itself.

III

> "The German workers' party, in order *to pave the way to the solution of the social question,* demands the establishment of producers' co-operative societies *with state aid under the democratic control of the toiling people.* The producers' co-operative societies *are to be called into being* for industry and agriculture on such a scale *that the socialist organization of the total labour will arise from them.*"

After the Lassallean "iron law of wages," the physic of the prophet. The way to it is "paved" in worthy fashion. In place of the existing class struggle there appears a newspaper scribbler's phrase, "the social *question*," to the "*solution*" of which one "paves the way." Instead of arising from the revolutionary process of transformation of society, the "socialist organization of the total labour" "arises" from the "state aid" that the state gives to the producers' co-operative societies and which the *state*, not the worker, "*calls into being*." It is worthy of Lassalle's imagination that a new society can be built with state loans just as well as a new railway!

From the remnants of a sense of shame, "state aid" has been put — under the democratic control of the "toiling people."

In the first place, the majority of the "toiling people" in Germany consists of peasants, and not of proletarians.

Secondly "democratic" means in German "*volksherrschaftlich*" ["by the rule of the people"]. But what does "control by the rule of the people of the toiling people" mean? And particularly in the case of a toiling people which, through these demands that it puts to the state, expresses its full consciousness that it neither rules nor is ripe for ruling!

It is superfluous to deal here with the criticism of the recipe prescribed by Buchez[20] in the reign of Louis Philippe[21] in *opposition* to the French Socialists and accepted by the reactionary workers of the *Atelier*.[22] The chief offence does not lie in having inscribed this specific nostrum in the programme, but in reverting, in general, from the standpoint of a class movement to that of a sectarian movement.

That the workers desire to establish the conditions for co-operative production on a social scale, and first of all on a national scale, in their own country, only means that they are working to revolutionize the present conditions of production, and it has nothing in common with the foundation of co-operative societies with state aid. But as far as the present co-operative societies are concerned, they are of value *only* in so far as they are the independent creations of the workers and not protégés either of the governments or of the bourgeois.

IV

I come now to the democratic section.

A. *"The free basis of the state."*

First of all, according to II, the German workers' party strives for "the free state."

Free state — what is this?

It is by no means the aim of the workers, who have got rid of the narrow mentality of humble subjects, to set the state free. In the German Empire the "state" is almost as "free" as in Russia. Freedom consists in converting the state from an organ standing above society into one completely subordinate to it, and today, too, the forms of state are more free or less free to the extent that they restrict the "freedom of the state."

The German workers' party — at least if it adopts the programme — shows that its socialist ideas are not even skin-deep; in that, instead of treating existing society (and this holds good for any future one) as the *basis* of the existing state (or of the future state in the case of future society), it treats the state rather as an independent entity that possesses its own "*intellectual, ethical and libertarian bases.*"

And what of the riotous misuse the programme makes of the words "*present-day state*," "*present-day society*," and of the still more riotous misconception it creates in regard to the state to which it addresses its demands?

"Present-day society" is capitalist society, which exists in all civilized countries, more or less free from medieval admixture, more or less modified by the special historical development of each country, more or less developed. On the other hand, the "present-day state" changes with a country's frontier. It is different in the Prusso-German Empire from what it is in Switzerland, it is different in England from what it is in the United States. "The present-day state" is, therefore, a fiction.

Nevertheless, the different states of the different civilized countries, in spite of their manifold diversity of form, all have this in common, that they are based on modern bourgeois society, only one more or less capitalistically developed. They have, therefore, also certain essential features in common. In this sense it is possible to speak of the "nature of the present-day state" [Staatswesen], in contrast with the future, in which its present root, bourgeois society, will have died off.

The question then arises: what transformation will the nature of the state [Staatswesen] undergo in communist society? In other words, what social functions will remain in existence there that are analogous to present functions of the state? This question can only be answered scientifically, and one does not get a flea-hop nearer to the problem by a thousandfold combination of the word people with the word state.

Between capitalist and communist society lies the period of the revolutionary transformation of the one into the other.

There corresponds to this also a political transition period in which the state can be nothing but *the revolutionary dictatorship of the proletariat.*

Now the programme does not deal with this nor with the nature of the future state [Staatswesen] of communist society.

Its political demands contain nothing beyond the democratic litany familiar to all: universal suffrage, direct legislation, popular rights, a people's militia, etc. They are a mere echo of the bourgeois People's Party, of the League of Peace and Freedom. They are all demands which, in so far as they are not exaggerated in fantastic presentation, have already been *realized.* Only the state to which they belong does not lie within the borders of the German Empire, but in Switzerland, the United States, etc. This sort of "state of the future" is a *present-day state,* although existing outside the "framework" of the German Empire.

But one thing has been forgotten. Since the German workers' party expressly declares that it acts within "the present-day national state," hence within *its own* state, the Prusso-German Empire — its demands would indeed otherwise be largely meaningless, since one only demands what one has not got — it should not have forgotten the chief thing, namely, that all those pretty little gewgaws rest on the recognition of the so-called sovereignty of the people and hence are appropriate only in a *democratic republic.*

Since one has not the courage — and wisely so, for the circumstances demand caution — to demand the democratic republic, as the French workers' programmes under Louis Philippe and under Louis Napoleon[23] did, one should not have resorted, either, to the subterfuge, neither "honest"[24] nor decent, of demanding things which have meaning only in a democratic republic from a state which is nothing but a police-guarded military despotism, embellished with parliamentary forms, alloyed with a feudal admixture, already influenced by the bourgeoisie and bureaucratically carpentered, and then to assure this state into the bargain that one imagines one will be able to force such things upon it "by legal means"!

Even vulgar democracy, which sees the millennium in the democratic republic and has no suspicion that it is precisely in this last form of state of bourgeois society that the class struggle has to be fought out to a conclusion — even it towers mountains above this kind of democratism within the limits of what is permitted by the police and not permitted by logic.

That, in fact, by the word "state" is meant the government machine, or the state in so far as it forms a special organism separated from society through division of labour, is shown by the words "the German workers' party demands *as the economic basis of the state*: a single progressive income tax," etc. Taxes are the economic basis of the government machinery and of nothing else. In the state of the future, existing in Switzerland, this demand has been pretty well fulfilled. Income tax presupposes the various sources of income of the various social classes, and hence capitalist society. It is, therefore, nothing remarkable that the Liverpool financial reformers, bourgeois headed by Gladstone's brother,[25] are putting forward the same demand as the programme.

B. "The German workers' party demands as the intellectual and ethical basis of the state:

1. "Universal and *equal elementary education* by the state. Universal compulsory school attendance. Free instruction."

Equal elementary education? What do these words suggest? Is it believed that in present-day society (and it is only with this one has to deal) education can be *equal* for all classes? Or is it demanded that the upper classes also shall be compulsorily reduced to the modicum of education — the elementary school — that alone is compatible with the economic conditions not only of the wage workers but of the peasants as well?

"Universal compulsory school attendance. Free instruction." The former exists even in Germany, the second in Switzerland and in the United States in the case of elementary schools. If in some states of the latter country higher educational institutions are also "free," that only means in fact defraying the cost of the education of the upper classes from the general tax receipts. Incidentally, the same holds good for "free administration of justice" demanded under A. 5. The administration of criminal justice is to be had free everywhere; that of civil justice is concerned almost exclusively with conflicts over property and hence affects almost exclusively the possessing classes. Are they to carry on their litigation at the expense of the national coffers?

The paragraph on the schools should at least have demanded technical schools (theoretical and practical) in combination with the elementary school.

"*Elementary education by the state*" is altogether objectionable. Defining by a general law the expenditures on the elementary schools, the qualifications of the teaching staff, the branches of instruction, etc., and, as is done in the United States, supervising the fulfilment of these legal specifications by state inspectors, is a very different thing from appointing the state as the educator of the people!

Government and church should rather be equally excluded from any influence on the school. Particularly, indeed, in the Prusso-German Empire (and one should not take refuge in the rotten subterfuge that one is speaking of a "state of the future"; we have seen how matters stand in this respect) the state has need, on the contrary, of a very stern education by the people.

But the whole programme, for all its democratic clang, is tainted through and through by the Lassallean sect's servile belief in the state, or, what is no better, by a democratic belief in miracles, or rather it is a compromise between these two kinds of belief in miracles, both equally remote from socialism.

"*Freedom of science*" says a paragraph of the Prussian constitution. Why, then, here?

"*Freedom of conscience!*" If one desired at this time of the *Kulturkampf*[26] to remind liberalism of its old slogans, it surely could have been done only in the following form: Everyone should be able to relieve his religious as well as his bodily needs without the police sticking their noses in. But the workers' party ought at any rate on this occasion to have expressed its awareness of the fact that bourgeois "freedom of conscience" is nothing but the toleration of all possible kinds of *religious freedom of conscience*, and that for its part it endeavours rather to liberate the conscience from the bogey of religion. But one chooses not to transcend the "bourgeois" level.

I have now come to the end, for the appendix that now follows in the programme does not constitute a characteristic component part of it. Hence I can be very brief here.

2. "*Normal working day.*"

In no other country has the workers' party limited itself to such an indefinite demand, but has always fixed the length of the working day that it considers normal under the given circumstances.

3. "Restriction of female labour and prohibition of child labour."

The standardization of the working day must include the restriction of female labour, in so far as it relates to the duration, intermissions, etc., of the working day; otherwise it could only mean the exclusion of female labour from branches of industry that are especially unhealthy for the female body or are objectionable morally for the female sex. If that is what was meant, it should have been said.

"*Prohibition of child labour!*" Here it was absolutely essential to state the age limit.

A *general prohibition* of child labour is incompatible with the existence of large-scale industry and hence an empty, pious wish. Its realization — if it were possible — would be reactionary, since, with a strict regulation of the working time according to the different age groups and other safety measures for the protection of children, an early combination of productive labour with education is one of the most potent means for the transformation of present-day society.

4. "State supervision of factory, workshop and domestic industry."

As against the Prusso-German state it should definitely have been demanded that the inspectors are to be removable only by a court of law; that any worker can have them prosecuted for neglect of duty; that they must belong to the medical profession.

5. "Regulation of prison labour."

A petty demand in a general workers' programme. In any case, it should have been clearly stated that there is no intention from fear of competition to allow ordinary criminals to be treated like beasts, and especially that there is no desire to deprive them of productive labour, their sole corrective. This was surely the least one might have expected from socialists.

6. "An effective liability law."

It should have been stated what is meant by an "effective" liability law.

Be it noted, incidentally, that in speaking of the normal working day the part of factory legislation that deals with health regulations and safety measures, etc., has been overlooked. The liability law only comes into operation when these regulations are infringed.

In short, this appendix also is distinguished by slovenly editing.

Dixi et salvavi animam mean [I have spoken and saved my soul].

ENGELS ON THE GOTHA PROGRAMME

ENGELS TO AUGUST BEBEL[27]

in Zwickau

London, March 18-28, 1875

Dear Bebel,

I received your letter of February 23 and am glad you are in such good health.

You ask me what we think of the unification business. Unfortunately our fate has been exactly the same as yours. Neither Liebknecht nor anyone else has sent us any information and we too, therefore, know only what is in the papers, and there was nothing in them until the draft programme appeared about a week ago! This draft has certainly astonished us not a little.

Our Party has so frequently made offers of reconciliation or at least of co-operation to the Lassalleans and has been so frequently and contemptuously repulsed by the Hasenclevers, Hasselmanns and Tölckes that any child must have drawn the conclusion: if these gentlemen are now coming and offering reconciliation themselves they must be in a damned tight fix. But considering the well-known character of these people it is our duty to utilize their fix in order to stipulate for every possible guarantee, so that they will not re-establish their impaired position in the public opinion of the workers at the expense of our Party. They should have been received with extreme coolness and mistrust, and union made dependent on the extent to which they were willing to drop their sectarian slogans and their state aid and to accept in its essentials the Eisenach programme of 1869[28] or an improved edition of it adapted to the present day. Our Party has *absolutely nothing to learn* from the Lassalleans in the theoretical sphere and therefore in what is decisive for the programme, but the Lassalleans certainly have something to learn from our Party; the first condition of union was that they should cease to be sectarians, Lassalleans, above all that the universal panacea of state aid should be, if not entirely relinquished, at any rate recognized by them as a subordinate transitional measure, one among and alongside of many other possible ones. The draft programme shows that our people are a hundred times superior theoretically to the Lassallean leaders — but to the same extent inferior to them in political cunning; the "honest" have been once more cruelly gypped by the dishonest.

In the first place Lassalle's high-sounding but historically false phrase is accepted: relatively to the working class all other classes are only one reactionary mass. This statement is only true in a few exceptional cases: for instance, in a revolution of the proletariat, like the Commune, or in a country where not only the bourgeoisie has moulded state and society in its own image but where in its wake the democratic petty bourgeoisie, too, has already carried out this remoulding down to its final consequences. If in Germany, for instance, the democratic petty bourgeoisie belonged to this reactionary mass, how could the Social-Democratic Workers' Party have gone hand in hand with it — with the People's Party — for years? How can the *Volksstaat*[29] take almost the whole of its political contents from the petty-bourgeois-democratic *Frankfurter Zeitung*?[30] And how can no less than seven demands be included in this programme which directly and literally coincide with the programme of the People's Party and the petty-bourgeois democracy? I mean the seven political demands, 1 to 5 and 1 to 2, of which there is not a single one that is not *bourgeois*-democratic.[31]

Secondly, the principle that the workers' movement is an international movement is, to all intents and purposes, completely disavowed for the present day, and that by the people who have upheld this principle most gloriously for five whole years under the most difficult conditions. The German workers' position at the head of the European movement is *essentially* based on their genuinely international attitude during the war; no other proletariat would have behaved so well. And now this principle is to be disavowed by them at the moment when the workers everywhere abroad are emphasizing it in the same degree as the governments are striving to suppress every attempted manifestation of it in an organization! And what is left of the internationalism of the workers' movement then? The faint prospect — not even of a future co-operation of the European workers for their emancipation — no, but of a future "international brotherhood of peoples," of the "United States of Europe" of the bourgeois of the Peace League![32]

It was of course quite unnecessary to speak of the International as such. But surely the very least was to make no retreat from the programme of 1869 and to say something to this effect: *although* the German workers' party is operating *first of all* within the state boundaries laid down for it (it has no right to speak in the name of the European proletariat and especially no right to say something false), it is conscious of its solidarity with the workers of all countries and will always be ready, in the future, as in the past, to fulfil the obligations imposed upon it by this solidarity. Such obligations exist even without exactly proclaiming or regarding oneself as a part of the International, for instance, help, abstention from blacklegging in strikes, care taken that the Party organs keep the German workers informed about the movement abroad, agitation against the threat or the outbreak of Cabinet-made wars, behaviour during such wars similar to that carried out in model fashion in 1870 and 1871, etc.

Thirdly, our people have allowed the Lassallean "iron law of wages" to be foisted upon them, a law based on a quite antiquated economic view, namely, that the worker receives on the average only the *minimum* in wages, and indeed because, according to Malthus' theory of population, there are always too many workers (this was Lassalle's argument). Now Marx has proved in detail in *Capital* that the laws regulating wages are very complicated, that sometimes one predominates and sometimes another, according to circumstances, that therefore they are in no sense iron but on the contrary very elastic, and that the matter can by no means be dismissed in a few words, as Lassalle imagined. The Malthusian argument in support of the law, which Lassalle copied from Malthus and Ricardo (with a distortion of the latter), as it is to be found, for instance, in the *Workers' Reader* [*Arbeiterlesebuch*], page 5,[33] quoted from another pamphlet of Lassalle's, has been refuted in detail by Marx in the section on the "Accumulation of Capital."[34] Thus by adopting Lassalle's "iron law" we commit ourselves to a false thesis with a false argument.

Fourthly, the programme puts forward as its *sole social* demand — Lassalle's state aid in its most naked form, as Lassalle stole it from Buchez. And this after Bracke has very well exposed[35] the utter futility of this demand and after almost all, if not all, our Party speakers have been obliged to come out against this "state aid" in fighting the Lassalleans! Lower than this our Party could not humiliate itself. Internationalism reduced to Amand Gögg[36] and socialism to the bourgeois republican Buchez, who put forward this demand *in opposition to the socialists*, in order to supplant them!

At the most, however, "state aid" in the Lassallean sense is only a *single* measure among many others designed to attain the end here lamely described as "paving the way to the solution of the social question," as if a theoretically *unsolved* social *question* still existed for us! So if one says: the German workers' party strives for the abolition of wage labour, and with it of class distinctions, by the establishment of co-operative production in industry and agriculture and on a national scale, and it supports every measure appropriate for the attainment of this end! — then no Lassallean can have anything against it.

Fifthly, there is not a word about the organization of the working class as a class by means of the trade unions. And that is a very essential point, for this is the real class organization of the proletariat, in which it carries on its daily struggles with capital, in which it trains itself, and which nowadays even amid the worst reaction (as in Paris at present) can simply no longer be smashed. Considering the importance which this organization has attained also in Germany, it would be absolutely necessary in our opinion to mention it in the programme and, where possible, to leave open a place for it in the Party organization.

All this has been done by our people to please the Lassalleans. And what has the other side conceded? That a heap of rather confused *purely democratic demands* should figure in the programme, of which several are a mere matter of fashion, as for instance, the "legislation by the people" which exists in Switzerland and does more harm than good if it does anything at all. *Administration* by the people, that would be something. Equally lacking is the first condition of all freedom: that all officials should be responsible for all their official acts to every citizen before the ordinary courts and according to common law. Of the fact that such demands as freedom of science and freedom of conscience figure in every liberal bourgeois programme and appear somewhat strange here, I shall say nothing more.

The free people's state is transformed into the free state. Taken in its grammatical sense, a free state is one where the state is free in relation to its citizens, hence a state with a despotic government. The whole talk about the state should be dropped, especially since the Commune, which was no longer a state in the proper sense of the word. The "people's state" has been thrown in our faces by the anarchists to the point of disgust, although already Marx's book against Proudhon[37] and later the *Communist Manifesto* directly declare that with the introduction of the socialist order of society the state will dissolve of itself [*sich von selbst auflöst*] and disappear. As, therefore, the state is only a transitional institution which is used in the struggle, in the revolution, in order to hold down one's adversaries by force, it is pure nonsense to talk of a free people's state: so long as the proletariat still *uses* the state, it does not use it in the interests of freedom but in order to hold down its adversaries, and as soon as it becomes possible to speak of freedom the state as such ceases to exist. We would therefore propose to replace *state* everywhere by "community" [*Gemeinwesen*], a good old German word which can very well represent the French word "*commune*."

"The elimination of all social and political inequality" is also a very questionable phrase in place of "the abolition of all class distinctions." Between one country and another, one province and another and even one locality and another there will always exist a *certain* inequality in the conditions of life, which it will be possible to reduce to a minimum but never entirely remove. Alpine dwellers will always have different conditions of life from those of people living on plains. The idea of socialist society as the realm of equality is a one-sided French idea resting upon the old "liberty, equality, fraternity," an idea which was justified as a *stage of development* in its own time and place but which, like all the one-sided ideas of the earlier socialist schools, should now be overcome, for they only produce confusion in people's heads and more precise modes of presentation of the matter have been found.

I shall stop, although almost every word in this, moreover, flatly and flaccidly written programme could be criticized. It is of such a character that if adopted Marx and I can *never* give our adherence to the *new* party established on this basis, and shall have very seriously to consider what our attitude towards it — in public as well — should be. You must remember that abroad *we* are made responsible for any and every utterance and action of the German

Social-Democratic Workers' Party. Thus Bakunin in his work *Statehood and Anarchy*, where we have to answer for every thoughtless word spoken or written by Liebknecht since the *Demokratisches Wochenblatt* was started.[38] People like to imagine that we run the whole business from here, while you know as well as I that we have hardly ever interfered in the least in internal Party affairs, and even then only in order to make good, so far as is possible, blunders, and *only theoretical* blunders, which have in our opinion been committed. But you will realize for yourself that this programme marks a turning point which may very easily compel us to refuse any and every responsibility for the Party which acknowledges it.

In general, the official programme of a party is of less importance than what the party does. But a *new* programme is after all a banner publicly raised, and the outside world judges the party by it. It should, therefore, on no account include a step backwards, as this one does in comparison with the Eisenach programme. One should also take into consideration what the workers of other countries will say to this programme, what impression will be produced by this bending of the knee to Lassalleanism on the part of the whole German socialist proletariat.

At the same time I am convinced that a union on *this* basis will not last a year. Are the best minds in our Party to lend themselves to grinding out repetitions, learnt by rote, of the Lassallean precepts on the iron law of wages and state aid? I should like to see you doing it, for instance! And if they did do this, they would be hissed down by their audiences. And I am sure the Lassalleans will insist on just *these* points of the programme like that usurer Shylock on his pound of flesh. The separation will come;

but we shall have made Hasselmann, Hasenclever, Tölcke and Co. "honest" again; we shall come out of the separation weaker and the Lassalleans stronger; our Party will have lost its political virginity and will never again be able to come out whole-heartedly against the Lassallean phrases which it will have inscribed for a time on its own banner; and if the Lassalleans then once more say that they are the most genuine, the only workers' party, while our people are bourgeois, the programme will be there to prove it. All the socialist measures in it are *theirs*, and all *our* Party has put into it are the demands of the petty-bourgeois democracy, which is nevertheless described *also by it* in the same programme as a part of the "reactionary mass."

I let this letter lie here as after all you are to be freed only on April 1, in honour of Bismarck's birthday,[39] and I did not want to expose it to the chance of being intercepted in any attempt to smuggle it in. And now a letter has just come from Bracke, who has also his grave doubts about the programme and wants to know our opinion. I am therefore sending this letter to him to be forwarded, so that he can read it and I need not write all this stuff over again. Moreover, I have also told the unvarnished truth to Ramm;[40] to Liebknecht I only wrote briefly. I do not forgive him for never telling us a *single word* about the whole thing (while Ramm and others thought he had given us exact information) until it was too late, so to speak. To be sure, this is what he has always done — hence the large amount of disagreeable correspondence which we, both Marx and I, have had with him; but this time it is really too bad and *we are certainly not going to co-operate.*

See that you manage to come here in the summer. You will, of course, stay with me, and if the weather is good we can go to the seaside for a couple of days, from which you will derive a lot of benefit after your long spell in jail.

Your friend,

F. E.

Marx has just moved. His new address is: No. 41, Maitland Park Crescent, N. W. London.

ENGELS TO WILHELM BRACKE

in Brunswick

122, Regent's Park Road
London, N. W.
October 11, 1875

Dear Bracke:

I have delayed answering your last letters (the last being that of June 28) up to now, first, because Marx and I were not together for six weeks — he was in Carlsbad and I was at the seaside, where I did not see the *Volksstaat* — and then, because I wanted to wait a little to see how the new unification and the combined committee[41] would behave in practice.

We are entirely of your opinion that Liebknecht has muddled the whole business in his zeal to obtain the unification and to pay *any* price for it. It might be considered necessary, but there was no need to say or show it to the other contracting party. After that, one mistake has always to be justified by another. After the Unity Congress had once been set going on a rotten basis and trumpeted abroad, it could not be allowed to fail at any price, and so one had to give way afresh on essential points. You are quite right: this unification bears within itself the seeds of a split, and I shall be glad if *only* the incurable fanatics fall away and not a whole retinue of otherwise able people it would be possible to make use of with good training. That will depend on the time when, and the circumstances in which, the inevitable takes place.

The programme in its final wording consists of three ingredients:

1. The Lassallean phrases and slogans, which should not have been accepted under any condition. If two fractions unite, they put in the programme what they agree on, not what is in dispute. But since our people conceded this, they voluntarily went through the Caudine Forks.[42]

2. A series of vulgar democratic demands, set out in the spirit and style of the People's Party.

3. A number of would-be communist principles, mostly borrowed from the *Manifesto* but so re-edited that on close inspection they one and all contain hair-raising nonsense. If one does not understand these matters, one should keep one's fingers off them or copy them literally from those who admittedly do understand the thing.

Fortunately, the programme has fared better than it deserves. The workers as well as the bourgeoisie and petty bourgeoisie read into it what should rightly be in it but is not, and it has not occurred to anyone from any side to investigate publicly a single one of these wonderful propositions for its real content. This has enabled us to keep silent about this programme. It comes to this, that nobody can translate these propositions into any foreign language without being *compelled* either to write down palpably crazy stuff or else, whether friend or foe, to inject a communist meaning into them. I myself have had to do so in a translation for our Spanish friends.

What I have seen of the activity of the committee is so far not gratifying. Firstly, the attack on your and B. Becker's writings;[43] through no fault of the committee, it did not prevail. Secondly, Sonnemann, whom Marx saw on his journey, reported that he had asked Vahlteich to be a *Frankfurter Zeitung* correspondent, but the committee had *forbidden* Vahlteich to accept the offer! Surely this even goes beyond censorship, and I cannot conceive how Vahlteich could allow himself to accept such a ban. And the clumsiness of it! Rather they should have seen to it that the *Frankfurter Zeitung* should be served by our people everywhere in Germany! Finally, the conduct of the Lassallean members in the establishment of the Association's Berlin printing house does not appear to me to be very honest either; while our people had in all confidence appointed the committee as the supervisory council in the case of the Leipzig printing house, those in Berlin had first to be *compelled* to do so. However, I do not know the details here exactly.

Meanwhile it is good that the committee is displaying little activity and confines itself, as C. Hirsch who was recently here says, to vegetating as a correspondence and information bureau. Any vigorous intervention on its part would only hasten the crisis, and people seem to sense this.

And what weakness, to accept three Lassalleans and two of our people on the committee!

Altogether, we seem to have come off with a black eye, and a big one at that. Let us hope that it rests at that, and that in the meantime propaganda has its effect among the Lassalleans. If the thing lasts until the next Reichstag elections,[44] it can be all right. But then Stieber and Tessendorf[45] will do their best, and the time will also come when it will be seen *what* has been taken over in Hasselmann and Hasenclever.

Marx has come back from Carlsbad quite changed, vigorous, fresh, cheerful and healthy, and can soon get down seriously to work again. He and I send you hearty greetings. When you have a chance, let us hear from you again how the business is going. The Leipzigers[46] are all too deeply interested in it to tell us the real truth, and the *internal* Party history cannot be made public, particularly just now.

Yours very sincerely,

F. E.

ENGELS TO AUGUST BEBEL

in Leipzig

London, October 12, 1875

Dear Bebel,

Your letter fully confirms our view that the unification was precipitate on our part and bears within itself the seeds of future disunion. It would be well if this disunion could be postponed until after the next Reichstag elections.

The programme, such as it is now, consists of three parts:

1. The Lassallean principles and slogans, the adoption of which remains a disgrace to our Party. When two fractions want to agree on a programme, they include what they agree on and do not touch upon what they disagree on. True, Lassallean state assistance was in the Eisenach programme, but as *one* of many *transitional measures* and, according to all I have heard, it would almost certainly have been thrown overboard, on Bracke's motion, at this year's Congress, *had it not been* for the unification. Now it figures as the sole and infallible panacea for all social ailments. It was an immense moral defeat for our Party to allow the

"iron law of wages" and other Lassallean phrases to be foisted upon it. It became converted to the Lassallean creed. That simply cannot be argued away. This part of the programme is the Caudine yoke under which our Party crawled to the greater glory of the holy Lassalle;

2. The democratic demands, which have been drawn up wholly in the spirit and style of the People's Party;

3. The demands on the "*present-day* state" (no one knows to whom the other "demands" are put), which are very confused and illogical;

4. General principles, mostly borrowed from the *Communist Manifesto* and the Rules of the International, but which have been so re-edited that they contain what is either *utterly false* or *pure bosh and nonsense*, as Marx has shown in detail in the essay known to you.

The whole thing is in the highest degree disorderly, confused, disconnected, illogical and discreditable. If the bourgeois press had possessed a single person of critical mind, he would have taken this programme apart sentence by sentence, investigated the real content of each phrase, demonstrated its nonsense with the utmost clarity, analysed its contradictions and economic howlers (for instance, that the instruments of labour are today "the monopoly of the capitalist class," as if there were no landowners; the talk about "the freeing of *labour*" instead of the freeing of the working class, as labour itself is indeed *much too free* nowadays) and made our whole Party look frightfully ridiculous. Instead, the asinine bourgeois papers took this programme quite seriously, read into it what it does not contain and interpreted it communistically. The workers seem to be doing the same. It is *this circumstance alone* that made it possible for Marx and me not to dissociate ourselves publicly from such a programme. So long as our opponents and likewise the workers inject our views into this programme, we may allow ourselves to keep quiet about it.

If you are satisfied with the result achieved in the question of personal composition, we must have sunk pretty low in our demands. Two of ours and three Lassalleans! So here too ours are not allies enjoying equal rights but vanquished elements outvoted from the very start. The activities of the committee, as far as we know them, are not edifying either: 1) Decision *not* to include in the list of Party literature Bracke's work and B. Becker's two works on Lassalleanism; if this decision is recalled it will not be the fault of the committee or of Liebknecht; 2) Instructions to Vahlteich forbidding him to accept the post of correspondent for the *Frankfurter Zeitung* offered him by Sonnemann. Sonnemann himself had told this to Marx, who met him on a trip. What surprises me even more than the arrogance of the committee and the readiness with which Vahlteich submitted instead of letting them go whistle is the enormous stupidity of this decision. The committee should rather have seen to it that a paper like the *Frankfurter Zeitung* is served everywhere *only* by our people. . . .

That the whole thing is an educational experiment which even under these circumstances promises to be very successful is something you are quite right about. The unification as such will be a great success if it lasts two years. But it undoubtedly was to be had much more cheaply. . . .

ENGELS TO KARL KAUTSKY

in Stuttgart

London, January 7, 1891

Dear Kautsky:[47]

Yesterday I sent you by registered mail Marx's manuscript which will have gladdened your heart. I doubt whether it can *thus* appear in the holy German Empire. Look it over from this angle and, where necessary, leave out the risky passages and replace them by dots. Where the context does not allow this, however, be so good as to indicate the places on the proof-sheets for me and, if possible, to tell me in a couple of lines the *reasons* why they are risky; I would then do whatever is possible. I would then put the changes in brackets and state in my introductory notes that these are *altered* passages. Therefore corrections on galley proofs, please!

Perhaps even people besides the high and mighty police will feel displeased over this publication. If you believe you have to be considerate on this account, I would beg of you to send the manuscript to Adler[48] *registered*. Over there in

Vienna it can probably be printed in its entirety (with the exception, alas, of the magnificent passage about relieving one's religious needs), *and printed it shall be in any case.* But I should think that my *very positive* intention which is herewith communicated to you completely covers you against any and every possible complaint. Since you people cannot prevent its publication, it is much better that it shall appear in Germany itself, and in the Party organ specifically established for such things, namely, *Die Neue Zeit.*

I have interrupted my work on Brentano[49] in order to get this manuscript ready for you; I must use the passages about the iron law of wages there too, and it was not worth the trouble not to get this ready for the printer at the same time. I had hoped to get through with Brentano this week, but so many upsets and letters have intervened that it will hardly be possible.

Well, if there are obstacles, be good enough to let me know. . . .

Yours,

F. Engels

ENGELS TO KARL KAUTSKY

in Stuttgart

London, January 15, 1891

Dear Baron:

You will see from the proof-sheets herewith enclosed that I am no brute and have even dispensed some tranquillizing morphine and potassium bromide in the introduction which ought to have a sufficiently soothing effect on the elegiac mood of our friend Dietz.[50] In addition, I shall write Bebel today. I didn't tell him about this matter earlier because I did not want to put him in a false position vis-à-vis Liebknecht. He would have been *obliged* to mention it to the latter, and Liebknecht, who had made extracts from the manuscript — as is proved by his speech on the Programme in Halle[51] — would have moved heaven and earth to prevent its publication.

If the passage "to relieve his religious *as well as his bodily* (needs)" cannot stay in, then cut out the words italicized and put dots in instead. The allusion becomes more delicate then, but it is still comprehensible enough.

After that it is to be hoped there will be no more misgivings.

Otherwise I have done everything you have asked for, in order to please you and Dietz and, as you can see, even *more*. . . .

Yours,

F. E.

ENGELS TO KARL KAUTSKY

in Stuttgart

London, February 3, 1891

Dear Kautsky:

You think we have been bombarded with letters on account of the Marx article — quite the contrary, we have heard and seen nothing.

When no *Neue Zeit* arrived on Saturday, I immediately thought something had happened again. On Sunday Ede[52] came and shared your letter with me. I thought then that the suppression plot had succeeded after all. At last, the issue arrived on Monday and after a little while I also discovered the reprint in *Vorwärts*.[53]

When punitive measures in the nature of the Anti-Socialist Law[54] failed, this bold leap was the best thing our people could do. But also it has the advantage that it fills a good part of the gap which can be bridged only with difficulty and which August[55] mentioned in his first fright. In any case, this fright was essentially based on the consideration: what will the enemy make of it? Since the thing was printed in the official organ, the exploitation by the enemy will be blunted and we put ourselves in a position where we can say: See how we criticize ourselves — we are the only party that can allow itself to do this; try and imitate us! And this is also the correct standpoint which should have been taken in the first place.

Consequently it also becomes hard for measures to be taken against you. My request to send the thing to Adler if need be was meant, on the one hand, to put pressure on Dietz, and on the other to cover your own responsibility, since to a certain extent I put you in a position where you had no choice. I also wrote August that I was taking the whole responsibility on myself alone.

If the responsibility otherwise falls on somebody else, it is on Dietz. He knows that I have always been very accommodating towards him in such matters. I have not only fulfilled all his wishes to tone down the language but have toned down even beyond his demands. Had he marked more, it would have still been taken into consideration. But why should I not let pass what Dietz did not take offence at?

For the rest, after their first fright most people except Liebknecht will be grateful to me for publishing the thing. It makes anything half-baked and all phrasemongering impossible in the next programme and supplies irrefutable arguments which most of them[56] would perhaps have hardly dared advance on their own initiative. It is no reproach that they did not change the bad programme under the Anti-Socialist Law because they could not do so. And now they themselves have given it up. They can now in fact admit without embarrassment that they acted clumsily during unification fifteen years ago and let Hasselmann, etc., hoodwink them. In any case, the three parts of the programme, namely: 1. specific Lassalleanism, 2. the vulgar democracy of the People's Party, and 3. nonsense, have not been improved by being preserved in vinegar for fifteen long years as the official Party programme, and if we dare not say this openly today, then when?

Let us know, please, if you hear anything new. Best regards.

Yours,

F. E.

ENGELS TO KARL KAUTSKY

in Stuttgart

London, February 11, 1891

Dear Kautsky:

Many thanks for both your letters. I herewith return those from Bebel and Schippel.

The Berliners' boycott of me has not been lifted, I hear and see nothing by letter, they are assuredly still undecided. On the other hand, the *Hamburger Echo*[57] had a very decent editorial, considering that those people are still very strongly imbued with Lassalleanism and even swear by the system of acquired rights.[58] Also I see from it and the *Frankfurter Zeitung* that the attacks of the enemy press are in full swing, if they have not already exhausted themselves. Once this has been overcome — and till now, as far as I can see, it was very mild — people will recover from their first fright. By contrast, Adler's Berlin correspondent (A. Braun?) formally thanks me for publishing.[59] A few more such voices, and resistance will flag.

It became clear to me that the manuscript was deliberately hidden and kept from Bebel in May/June 1875 as soon as he gave me April 1 as the date of his release from prison; I have also written him that he *must* have seen it in the absence of "anything untoward." If necessary, I shall ask him for a reply to this. For a long time the document was in the hands of Liebknecht, from whom Bracke only got it back with difficulty; Liebknecht wanted to keep it entirely to himself in order to use it in the final editing of the programme. How, is now quite clear.

Please send me the manuscript of Lafargue's[60] article registered in a paper-wrapper, and I shall no doubt put the matter in order. By the way, his article on Padlewski was quite good and very useful in the face of the *Vorwärts* distortions regarding French policy. In this, Wilhelm[61] is altogether out of luck. *He* puffs the French Republic everywhere, and his specially engaged correspondent, Guesde, pulls it down all over the lot.[62]

Schippel's announcement about the fraction's explanation[63] leaves me utterly cold. If they so wish, I am ready to confirm to them that I am not used to asking for their permission. It is all the same to me whether this pleases them or not. I willingly grant them the right to pronounce their adverse opinion on this or that. I don't dream of replying unless the matter comes to such a pass that I am absolutely forced to deal with it. So let's wait.

On this account, too, I shall not write to Bebel, first, because he himself must tell me what sort of final opinion he has formed on the matter and, second, because every resolution of the fraction is signed by all, whether they voted for it or not. Furthermore, Bebel is wrong if he believes I shall allow myself to be driven into an acrimonious polemic. For that, however, they would first have to come at me with untruths, etc., which I could not possibly let pass. On the contrary, I am indeed soaked through and through with conciliatoriness, I really have no reason to be angry and am burning with the craving to build any bridge — a pontoon, a trestle bridge, an iron or stone bridge, even a golden one — over the possible abyss or rift suspected from afar by Bebel.

Strange! Schippel now writes of the many old Lassalleans who are proud of their Lassallery — and when they were here,[64] it was unanimously stated: There are no more Lassalleans in Germany! This was actually one of the main reasons which dissipated my many misgivings. And here comes Bebel too and thinks that a great number of the best comrades have been badly hurt. But then they should have [told] me how things stood.

Besides, if now after fifteen years one cannot talk straightforwardly about Lassalle's theoretical nonsense and his acting the prophet, then when should one?

But the Party itself, the executive, the fraction and *tutti quanti* (all the others) are shielded by the Anti-Socialist Law from all blame, except that they accepted such a programme (and this cannot be avoided). As long as the Law was in force, any revision was out of the question. As soon as this ended, revision was put on the agenda. So what more does one want?

And it is also necessary that people finally stop treating Party functionaries — their own servants — with the eternal kid gloves and standing most obediently instead of critically before them, as if they were infallible bureaucrats.

Yours,

F. E.

ENGELS TO FREDERICK ADOLF SORGE

in Hoboken

London, February 11, 1891

Dear Sorge:

Received your letter of January 16. . . .

You have read Marx's article in the *Neue Zeit*. The great anger it first caused among the socialist bosses in Germany seems to be abating now. In the Party itself, however — with the exception of the old Lassalleans — there was much rejoicing. The Berlin correspondent of the Vienna *Arbeiter-Zeitung*,[65] which you will receive by the *next* mail (I think it's Adolf Braun, Victor Adler's brother-in-law and Liebknecht's sub-editor on the *Vorwärts)*, formally thanks me for the service I have rendered the Party. Liebknecht, of course, is raging, since the whole Critique is specifically aimed at him and he is the father of the rotten programme which he begot with that bugger Hasselmann. I understand the initial horror of those people who had hitherto insisted that they should be treated ever so gently by the "comrades" when now they are handled *sans façon* (unceremoniously) and their programme is revealed as pure nonsense. As Karl Kautsky who has acted very courageously in the whole matter writes me, there is a plan to release a fraction edict to the effect that the publication took place without their prior knowledge and that they disapproved of it. They can willingly have the fun. But even this may not happen, if assent increases within the Party and they find the clamour that "a weapon against us ourselves has thus been put in the enemy's hands" is not worth much.

In the meantime, I am boycotted by these gentlemen, which is quite all right with me, since it saves me wasting a lot of time. It won't last too long anyway. . . .

Yours,

F. E.

ENGELS TO KARL KAUTSKY[66]

in Stuttgart

London, February 23, 1891

Dear Kautsky,

You will have received my hasty congratulations of the day before yesterday. So now to return again to the matter in hand, Marx's letter.[67]

The fear that it would put a weapon in the hands of our opponents was unfounded. Malicious insinuations, of course, are being attached to anything and everything, but on the whole the impression made on our opponents was one of complete bewilderment at this ruthless self-criticism and the feeling: what an inner power must be possessed by a party that can afford such a thing! That can be seen from the hostile newspapers you sent me (for which many thanks) and from those to which I have otherwise had access. And, frankly speaking, that really was my intention when I published the document. I was aware of the fact that at the first moment some persons here and there would be most unpleasantly affected by it, but this was inevitable, and it was amply outweighed, in my view, by the contents of the document. I knew, also, that the Party was quite strong enough to stand it, and I reckoned that it would today also be able to stomach this unconcealed language used fifteen years ago; that one would point with justifiable pride to this test of strength and would say: Where is there another party that can dare the like? That has been left, meanwhile, to the Saxon and Vienna *Arbeiter-Zeitung* and to the *Züricher Post.*[68]

It is very nice of you that in No. 21 of the *Neue Zeit* you take upon yourself the responsibility for the publication;[69] but do not forget that, after all, I gave the first impulse and moreover to a certain extent I put you in a position in which you had no choice. I claim, therefore, the main responsibility for myself. As far as details are concerned, one can certainly always have different opinions about them. I have deleted and altered everything that you and Dietz have objected to, and if Dietz had marked even more I would still, as far as possible, have been amenable even then; of that I have always given you proof. But, as far as the main point is concerned, it was *my duty* to publish the thing once the programme had come up for discussion. And especially now, after Liebknecht's report in Halle, in which he utilizes his extracts from it in part unceremoniously as his own property, and in part as objects of attack without mentioning the source, Marx would certainly have confronted this rehash with the original and it was my duty in his place to do the same. Unfortunately, at that time I had not yet got the document; I only found it considerably later after much search.

You say that Bebel writes to you that Marx's treatment of Lassalle has caused bad blood among the old Lassalleans.

That may be so. People, you see, do not know the real story and nothing appears to have happened to enlighten them about it. If these people do not know that Lassalle's whole greatness rests on this, that for years Marx allowed him to parade the results of Marx's research as his own and, owing to defective education in economics, to distort them into the bargain, then that is not my fault. But I am Marx's literary executor and as such I have my duty to perform.

Lassalle has belonged to history for twenty-six years. While under the Exceptional Law historical criticism of him has been left in abeyance, the time is at last at hand when it must have its say and Lassalle's position in relation to Marx be made plain. The legend that conceals and glorifies the true image of Lassalle can surely not become an article of faith of the Party. However highly one may estimate Lassalle's services to the movement, his historical role in it remains an equivocal one. Lassalle the socialist is accompanied step by step by Lassalle the demagogue. Everywhere, Lassalle, the conductor of the Hatzfeldt law suit,[70] shows through Lassalle the agitator and organizer: the same cynicism in choice of means, the same preference for surrounding himself with suspicious and corrupt people who can be used as mere tools and discarded. Until 1862 a specifically Prussian vulgar democrat in practice, with strong Bonapartist leanings (I have just looked through his letters to Marx), he suddenly switched round for purely personal reasons and began his agitation; and before two years had gone by he was demanding that the workers should take the part of the monarchy against the bourgeoisie, and intriguing with Bismarck, akin to him in character, in a way that would certainly have led to the actual betrayal of the movement, if fortunately for him he had not been shot in time. In his agitational writings, the correct things that he borrowed from Marx are so much interwoven with his own Lassallean, invariably false expositions that the two are hardly to be separated. The section of the workers that feels itself injured by Marx's judgement knows Lassalle only through his two years of agitation, and even these only through coloured spectacles. But historical criticism cannot stand eternally, hat in hand, before such prejudices. It was my duty finally to settle accounts between Marx and Lassalle. That has been done. For the time being I can content myself with that. Moreover, I myself have other things to do now. And Marx's published ruthless judgement of Lassalle will by itself have its effect and give others courage. But should I be forced to it, there would be no choice for me: I should have to clear away the Lassalle legend once for all.

That voices have been raised in the Reichstag group saying that the *Neue Zeit* should be placed under censorship is indeed a fine affair. What is this, the ghost of the Reichstag group's dictatorship during the Anti-Socialist Law (which was, of course, necessary and excellently carried out), or is it due to remembrance of von Schweitzer's[71] whilom strict organization? It is indeed a brilliant idea to put German socialist science, after its liberation from Bismarck's Anti-Socialist Law, under a new Anti-Socialist Law to be manufactured and carried out by the Social-Democratic Party authorities themselves. For the rest, it is ordained that trees shall not grow into the sky.

The article in the *Vorwärts* does not stir me much. I shall wait for Liebknecht's account of what happened and shall then reply to both in as friendly a tone as possible.

In the *Vorwärts* article there are only a few inaccuracies to be corrected (for example, that we did not desire unity, that events proved Marx wrong, etc.) and a few obvious things to be confirmed. With this answer I intend then, for my part, to close the discussion unless new attacks or false assertions compel me to continue.

Tell Dietz that I am working on the *Origin*.[72] But today Fischer writes to me and wants three new prefaces as well![73]

Yours,

F. E.

ENGELS TO FREDERICK ADOLF SORGE

in Hoboken

London, March 4, 1891

Dear Sorge:

Received your letter of February 19. In the meantime you probably have heard much more about the Social-Democratic fraction's great indignation concerning the publication of Marx's letter about the Programme in the *Neue Zeit*. The matter is still in progress. For the time being, I let those people make fools of themselves, and for that matter Liebknecht has perpetrated some dubious things in the *Vorwärts*. Naturally I shall reply in due course, but without unnecessary squabbling, although this may well be scarcely possible without some light irony. Of course, all the people who count theoretically are on my side — with the sole exception of Bebel, who in fact is not without cause in feeling I have hurt him — but that was unavoidable. I have not been able to look at the *Volkszeitung*[74] for four weeks because of overwork and therefore do not know whether the reflected lightning has struck in America — the remnants of Lassalleanism are foaming in Europe, and you have enough of them there, too. . . .

Yours,

F. E.

ENGELS TO AUGUST BEBEL

in Berlin

London, May 1-2, 1891

Dear Bebel:

I am replying today to your two letters of March 30 and April 25.[75] It was with great joy that I read your silver wedding went so well and made you look forward to your golden one. I wish with all my heart that you may both live to see it. We need you for a long time yet after the devil has taken me — to use Old Dessauer's words.

I must return to Marx's Critique of the Programme, I hope for the last time. I must deny that "*nobody* would have objected to the publication in itself." Liebknecht would *never* have voluntarily agreed to it and would have done his utmost to prevent it. Since 1875 this Critique has stuck in his craw to such an extent that he thinks of it the moment there is talk of a "programme." His whole speech at Halle hinges on this subject. His puffed up *Vorwärts* article is simply an expression of his bad conscience about this selfsame Critique. And indeed it is in the first place directed against him. We regarded him as the father of the Unity Programme — in its rotten aspect, and I still do so. And that was the point which determined my unilateral action. Had I been able to thrash the matter out with you alone and then send it off immediately to Karl Kautsky for printing, we could have reached agreement in two hours. But then I considered you to be obliged — personally and from a Party viewpoint — to discuss it with Liebknecht also. And then I knew the outcome. Either suppression or an open row, at least for some time, even with you, if I still went ahead. The following proves that I was not wrong: Since you came out of clink on April 1 [1875] and the document is dated only May 5, it is clear — until further elucidation — that the thing was *deliberately kept* from you, and this can have happened *only through Liebknecht.* But for the sake of sweet peace you have let him send the lie out into the world that you didn't get to see the thing because you were in jail. And so you would have had consideration for him even before publication in order to avoid a scandal in the executive. I find this understandable too, but I hope you too will understand that I had to consider that in all probability things would have been handled in this way.

I have just been looking the thing over again. Perhaps some more could have been left out without harm to the whole. But surely not *much.* What was the situation? We knew as well as you and as, for instance, the *Frankfurter Zeitung* of March 9, '75, which I happened to find, that the *matter was decided* with the acceptance of the draft by your plenipotentiaries. Thus Marx wrote the thing only to absolve his conscience and without any hope of success; *dixi et salvavi animam meam* (I have spoken and saved my soul) is written in evidence underneath. And Liebknecht's bluster with the "categorical no" is therefore nothing but vain boasting, and he knows it too. Since you people blundered in the choice of your representatives and then had to swallow the programme so as not to let the whole unification come to grief, you surely cannot object if the warning which had reached you before the final decision was taken is published now, *after fifteen years!* This stamps you neither as blockheads nor as cheats, unless you claim infallibility for your official actions.

To be sure, you yourself had not read the warning. But that also has been published and so you are in an exceptionally favourable position, as compared with those who did read it and still acquiesced in the draft.

I hold the covering letter to be very important. For the only correct policy is explained in it. Parallel action during a period of probation, that was the only thing which could have saved you from bartering away principles. But Liebknecht was unwilling at any price to forego the glory of having brought about unification, and yet it is a miracle that he did not go even further in his concessions. From bourgeois democracy he has brought over and maintained a real mania for unification.

That the Lassalleans came because they *had to*, because their whole party was falling to pieces, because their leaders were either scoundrels or donkeys whom the masses were no longer willing to follow, all this can be said today in well-chosen, mild words. As a matter of course their "tight organization" ended in complete dissolution. It is therefore ridiculous when Liebknecht excuses the acceptance en bloc of the Lassallean creed on the ground that the Lassalleans sacrificed their tight organization — there was nothing left to be sacrificed!

Do you wonder where the obscure and confused phrases in the programme come from? But they are all precisely Liebknecht incarnate, the phrases over which we have quarrelled with him for years and with which he is infatuated. He has always been confused theoretically, and to this day our sharp formulation is an abomination to him. On the other hand, as an old People's Party member he still loves high-sounding phrases which can mean everything possible or nothing at all. Since confused Frenchmen, Englishmen and Americans in those days spoke of the "emancipation of labour" instead of that of the working *class* because they did not know any better, and since the language of the people being spoken to had to be used even here and there in the documents of the International, this was reason enough for Liebknecht to put the screws on the German Party to force it back to the same vanquished standpoint in its modes of expression. And it is absolutely impossible to say that he did this "against his own better knowledge," since he really did not know any better then, and I am not sure whether this does not also apply today. At any rate, he is forever falling back into the old vague modes of expression even today — of course, they are easier to use rhetorically. And since he cared at least as much for the basic democratic demands he thought he understood as for the economic principles he did not clearly understand, he was surely honest when he thought he had concluded a brilliant deal by bartering democratic staples for Lassallean dogmas.

As for the attacks on Lassalle, these were among the most important things to me, as I have said. By accepting *all* the essential Lassallean economic phrases and demands the Eisenachers *actually became Lassalleans*, at least according to the programme. The Lassalleans had sacrificed nothing, absolutely nothing, which they could have retained. To complete the latter's victory, you accepted as your Party song the moralizing rhymed prose with which Herr Audorf commemorates Lassalle.[76] And during the thirteen years of the Anti-Socialist Law it was self-evidently impossible to stand up to the cult of Lassalle inside the Party. This had to be terminated, and this I have instigated. I shall no longer allow Lassalle's spurious fame to be maintained and proclaimed anew *at Marx's expense.* The people who personally knew and idolized Lassalle have thinned out, and among all the others the cult of Lassalle is *purely fabricated*, fabricated by our silent toleration against our better knowledge and therefore without even the justification of a personal attachment. The inexperienced people and the newcomers have been adequately taken into consideration by the publication of the thing *in the "Neue Zeit."* But I can in no wise concede that in such matters historical truth must step back — after fifteen years of lamb-like patience — in favour of convenience and because of the possibility of giving offence inside the Party. At all such times it is inevitable that some good people get hurt. And that thereupon they grumble. And if they then say that Marx was envious of Lassalle, and if German papers and even (!!) the Chicago *Vorbote*[77] (which writes for a greater number of specific Lassalleans — in Chicago — than exist in all Germany) join the chorus, it affects me less than a flea-bite. We have had altogether different things thrown at our heads and have still got on with the agenda. There is the example of Marx handling Saint Ferdinand Lassalle roughly and that is enough for the moment.

And now one more thing: Since you people are trying to stop publication of the article by force and have sent warnings to the *Neue Zeit* that the Party would turn it into Party property and put it under censorship if such things happened again, the Party's taking possession of your whole press must needs appear in a strange light to me. How do you distinguish yourselves from Puttkamer if you introduce an Anti-Socialist Law into your own ranks? This is really immaterial to me personally, no party in any country can condemn me to silence if I am determined to speak. But I would like you to consider whether you might not do better by being less sensitive and somewhat less — Prussian — in your behaviour. You — the Party — *needs* socialist science, which cannot exist without freedom of movement. For that, one has to put up with inconveniences, and it's best to do so with grace, without flinching. Even a slight tension, not to speak of a rift, between the German Party and German socialist science would be a misfortune and an unparalleled disgrace. It is self-evident that the executive and you personally maintain, and must maintain, an important *moral* influence on the *Neue Zeit* as well as on everything else being published. But that must suffice for you and it can, too. The *Vorwärts* is always boasting about the inviolable freedom of discussion, but one does not see much of it. You just don't know how strange such a propensity to coercive measures appears here abroad, where one is accustomed to seeing the oldest party chiefs duly called to account in their own party (for instance, the Tory government by Lord Randolph Churchill). And then you must also not forget that in a big party discipline can by no means be so tight as in a small sect, and that the Anti-Socialist

Law which hammered the Lassalleans and the Eisenachers together (although according to Liebknecht, his splendid programme really achieved this!) and made such close cohesion necessary no longer exists. . . .

F. E.

NOTES

[1] Marx's *Critique of the Gotha Programme* is one of the most important contributions to the development of the theory of scientific communism and an example of uncompromising struggle against opportunism. It was written in April and early May of 1875 and sent to the leadership of the Eisenachers (Wilhelm Bracke) on May 5, 1875. The work contains a critical examination of the draft programme of the united German Social-Democratic Party and was prepared for the Gotha Unity Congress.

The *Critique of the Gotha Programme* was first published by Engels in 1891 despite the opposition of the opportunist leadership of the German Social-Democratic Party. It appeared, together with Engels' "Foreword," in *Die Neue Zeit*, the theoretical organ of the German Social-Democratic Party, Vol. 1, No. 18, 1891.

Engels also published Marx's relevant letter to Wilhelm Bracke of May 5, 1875, together with the *Critique of the Gotha Programme.*

It is clear from Engels' letter to Karl Kautsky of February 23, 1891, that Engels had to agree to tone down some of the more incisive passages. The present edition is a verbatim translation from Marx's manuscript. p. 1

[2] At the Gotha Congress, which took place from May 22 to 27, 1875, the two existing German workers' organizations — the Social-Democratic Workers' Party (the Eisenachers) founded by Liebknecht and Bebel in Eisenach in 1869 and led by them, and the Lassallean General Association of German Workers headed by Hasenclever, Hasselmann and Tölcke — united to form the Socialist Workers' Party of Germany. p. 3

[3] The Congress of the German Social-Democratic Party at Halle — the first after the repeal of the Anti-Socialist Law — decided on October 16, 1890, on the motion of Wilhelm Liebknecht, the main author of the

Gotha Programme, to prepare a new draft programme for the next Party congress. This new programme was adopted in October of the following year at the Erfurt Congress (the Erfurt Programme). p. 3

[4] The Hague Congress of the First International, held in September 1872, was marked by the struggle against Bakunin. The majority at the congress supported the stand of the General Council led by Marx. Bakunin was expelled from the International. p. 4

[5] Bakunin's *Statehood and Anarchy*, Zurich, 1873. p. 6

[6] The People's Party of Germany, established in 1865, consisted mainly of petty-bourgeois democrats from the South German states and a section of the bourgeois democrats. It opposed the hegemony of Prussia over Germany and advanced general democratic slogans which also reflected the secessionist tendency of some German states. It advocated building a German federation and opposed unifying Germany under a centralized democratic republic.

In 1866, the People's Party of Saxony, which had workers as its nucleus, merged with the German People's Party, forming its left wing. The combined Party agreed to settling the question of national unification by democratic means and later developed in a socialist direction. After breaking with the petty-bourgeois democrats, it participated in founding the Social-Democratic Workers' Party in August 1869. p. 6

[7] The Unity Congress of German Social-Democracy was held on May 22-27, 1875, in Gotha; the congress of the Lassalleans had taken place earlier in May, while the congress of the Eisenachers was convened afterwards, on June 8, in Hamburg. p. 6

[8] The first French translation of Volume I of *Capital*, which Marx himself edited, was published in instalments in 1872-75 in Paris. p. 7

[9] The publishing house of the Social-Democratic Workers' Party attached to the editorial board of *Volksstaat* (*People's State*), the central organ of the party. p. 7

[10] The second edition of Marx's pamphlet, *Revelations About the Cologne Communist Trial* (Karl Marx and Frederick Engels, *Works*, German ed., Vol. 8, pp. 405-70). It was issued in 1875 by the *Volksstaat* bookshop at Leipzig. p. 7

[11] Karl Marx and Frederick Engels, *Manifesto of the Communist Party*, Foreign Languages Press, Peking, 1970, p. 44. p. 19

[12] The Reichstag elections of January 10, 1874. p. 19

[13] "The Marat of Berlin" is an ironic reference to Hasselmann, the chief editor of *Neuer Sozialdemokrat*.

The magazine *Neuer Sozialdemokrat* was the organ of the Lassallean General Association of German Workers, appearing three times a week in Berlin from 1871 to 1876. It pursued a line which faithfully reflected the Lassallean policy of accommodation to the Bismarck regime and propitiation of the German ruling classes, as well as the Lassallean leadership's opportunism and nationalism. Adopting a sectarian stand, it consistently opposed the Marxist leadership of the International and the German Social-Democratic Workers' Party, and supported the hostile activities of the Bakuninists and other anti-proletarian elements against the General Council of the International. p. 20

[14] The International League of Peace and Freedom was a bourgeois pacifist organization set up in Switzerland in 1867 by a group of petty-bourgeois Republicans and liberals (Victor Hugo, Giuseppe Garibaldi, and others taking an active part in it). In 1867-68 Mikhail Bakunin joined in the work of the League. During its early period, the League attempted to use the working class movement to attain its own ends. It asserted that war could be eliminated through the establishment of a "United States of Europe," thus spreading illusions among the masses in order to divert the proletariat from class struggle. p. 21

[15] After the fall of the Paris Commune, Bismarck attempted in 1871-72 to conclude a formal treaty with Austria and Russia for united action against the revolutionary movement in general, and against the First International in particular. In accordance with Bismarck's proposal, the Three Emperors' League of Germany, Russia and Austria-Hungary was formed in October 1873 to take common action once a "European disturbance" occurred. p. 21

[16] The *Norddeutsche Allgemeine Zeitung* editorial of March 20, 1875, on the draft programme. It stated that "Social-Democratic agitation has in some respects become more prudent: it is renouncing the International."

Norddeutsche Allgemeine Zeitung (*North-German General Newspaper*), a reactionary daily published in Berlin from 1861 to 1918, was the organ of the Bismarck government from the sixties to the eighties. p. 22

[17] Lassalle formulated this law as, "The iron economic law which, under present-day conditions, *under the rule of the supply and demand of labour*, determines wages is this: that the average wage always remains reduced to the necessary subsistence level which in any given nation is habitually needed for eking out a living and for propagation.

"It is the pivot around which the actual daily wage constantly swings pendulum-like, without ever rising above it or falling below it for long. The actual daily wage cannot remain above this average for any length of time, otherwise the lightened, improved condition of the workers would give rise to an increase of the working population and, consequently, of the supply of factory hands, which in turn would bring wages down to the original level or below.

"Wages cannot remain far below this necessary subsistence level for long, because this would cause migration, celibacy, abstention from producing children and thus finally reduction in the number of workers due to poverty, whereby the supply of factory hands would be lowered and wages would return to their original higher level. The actual average wage is, therefore, destined to be always fluid, to fluctuate around this pivot to which it must constantly return, to be sometimes above and sometimes below it" (*Arbeiterlesebuch* [*Workers' Reader*], two speeches by Lassalle in Frankfort-on-Main on May 17 and 19, 1863, Hottingen-Zurich, 1887).

Lassalle first explained this "law" in his pamphlet "An Open Answer to the Central Committee for Convening a General Congress of German Workers at Leipzig" (Zurich, 1863, pp. 15-16). p. 22

[18] A quotation from Goethe's "Das Göttliche." p. 22

[19] The theory advanced by Friedrich Albert Lange (1828-75) in his work *Die Arbeiterfrage in ihrer Bedeutung für Gegenwart und Zukunft* (*The Labour Question: Its Significance for the Present and the Future*), Duisburg, 1865, pp. 144-61 and 180. p. 22

[20] Philippe Joseph Buchez (1796-1865), French historian and publicist. In the 1840s he advocated French Catholic socialism, which demanded the formation of producers' co-operative societies with state aid. p. 25

[21] Louis Philippe (1773-1850), King of France in the period of the "July Monarchy." He ascended the throne after the July Revolution of 1830, and the February Revolution of 1848 brought his reign to an end. p. 25

[22] *L'Atelier* (*Workshop*), a monthly published in Paris from 1840 to 1850 by artisans and workers influenced by Catholic socialism. Its editorial board included workers' representatives who were re-elected every three months. p. 25

[23] Napoleon III (Louis Bonaparte), Emperor of France (1852-70). p. 28

[24] "Honest" was the epithet applied to the Eisenachers. p. 28

[25] Robert Gladstone, a Liverpool merchant and liberal who advocated a progressive income tax which should fall primarily on the big landowners. He was the brother of William Gladstone (1809-98), British Liberal Prime Minister in the last half of the 19th century. p. 29

[26] "Kulturkampf" (struggle for culture), a term applied by bourgeois liberals to the legal measures adopted by the Bismarck government in the 1870s. Under the pretext of fighting for secular culture, they were aimed against Catholicism and the party of the "Centre" which supported the secessionism and anti-Prussian tendency of the officials, landowners and bourgeoisie of the medium-sized and smaller southwest German states. However, in the 1880s, Bismarck repealed most of these measures in order to muster all the reactionary forces of the states. p. 31

[27] This letter is closely related in content to Marx's *Critique of the Gotha Programme* and expresses Marx's and Engels' common view on the union of the two German workers' parties which was planned for early 1875. The immediate reason for this letter was the publication in *Volksstaat* and in *Neuer Sozialdemokrat*, March 7, 1875, of the draft programme of the would-be united German Social-Democratic Workers' Party. The draft was revised only slightly and adopted at the Unity Gotha Congress of May 1875. It has since been known as the Gotha Programme.

Marx and Engels favoured merging the two workers' parties. However, they held that the unification was possible only on the basis of sound principles. In his letter to Bebel, Engels criticized the draft and warned the Eisenachers not to give in to the Lassalleans. Not until 36 years later was the letter first published in Bebel's book *Aus meinem Leben* (*From My Life*), Part 2, Stuttgart, 1911. p. 37

[28] The programme adopted at the General German Social-Democratic Workers' Congress at Eisenach on August 7-9, 1869, which was attended by German, Austrian and Swiss Social-Democrats. The German Social-Democratic Workers' Party, later known as the Eisenach party, was founded at this congress. The Eisenach Programme adhered in general to the line of the International. p. 38

[29] *Der Volksstaat*, central organ of the German Social-Democratic Workers' Party (Eisenachers), published in Leipzig from October 2, 1869, to September 29, 1876, twice weekly at first, then three times a week from July 1873. The journal represented the viewpoint of the revolutionaries in the German working-class movement and was therefore subjected to frequent persecution by the government and police. As the editors were arrested from time to time, the editorial board membership was always changing, but the leadership of the paper remained in the hands of Wilhelm Liebknecht. August Bebel also played a prominent role. Marx and Engels had been contributors since the journal's founding and often helped the editorial board. p. 39

[30] The *Frankfurter Zeitung* was the shortened name of the *Frankfurter Zeitung und Handelsblatt*, originally a daily with a petty-bourgeois democratic orientation, published from 1856 to 1943 at Frankfort-on-Main. p. 39

[31] These political demands of the draft Gotha Programme read as follows:

The German Workers' Party demands as the free basis of the state:

1. Universal, equal, direct and secret suffrage for all males twenty-one years of age and above, in all elections — national and local. 2. Direct legislation by the people with the right of initiating and vetoing proposals. 3. Universal military training; people's militia to replace the standing army. Questions of war and peace to be decided by the representative assembly of the people. 4. Abolition of all exceptional laws, especially the laws on the press, association and assembly. 5. People's courts. Free administration of justice.

The German Workers' Party demands as the intellectual and moral basis of the state:

1. Universal and equal elementary education by the state. Universal compulsory school attendance. Free instruction. 2. Freedom of science. Freedom of conscience. p. 39

[32] *I.e.*, the International League of Peace and Freedom. See Note 14. p. 39

[33] See Note 17. p. 40

[34] See Karl Marx, *Capital*, Vol. I, Part VII. p. 41

[35] Wilhelm Bracke's *Der Lassalle'sche Vorschlag* (*The Lassallean Proposal*), Brunswick, 1873. p. 41

[36] Amand Gögg (1820-97), one of the leaders of the bourgeois League of Peace and Freedom. p. 41

[37] Marx's *The Poverty of Philosophy* (Karl Marx and Frederick Engels, *Works*, German ed., Vol. 4, pp. 63-182). p. 42

[38] *Demokratisches Wochenblatt* (*Democratic Weekly*), a German workers' journal published from January 1868 to September 1869 in Leipzig under the editorship of Wilhelm Liebknecht. In December 1868 it became the organ of the Union of German Workers' Associations led by August Bebel. In the beginning the journal was to some extent influenced by the petty-bourgeois ideology of the People's Party. But thanks to Marx's and Engels' efforts, it began to conduct the struggle against the Lassalleans and to spread the ideas of the International and publish its important documents, so that it played a significant role in the founding of the

German Social-Democratic Workers' Party. At the Eisenach Party Congress in 1869 it was renamed the party's central organ and its title was changed to *Der Volksstaat* (see Note 29). p. 44

[39] On account of the revolutionary-internationalist position they adopted during the Franco-Prussian War of 1870-71, Liebknecht and Bebel were charged with treason at the famous Leipzig trial in March 1872 and sentenced to two years' imprisonment in a fortress. Bebel's term expired on May 14, 1874, but six weeks later he was again jailed in Zwickau, Saxony, for another nine months, for "lèse majesté." He was finally released on April 1, 1875, coincidentally Bismarck's birthday. p. 45

[40] Hermann Ramm, one of the editors of *Der Volksstaat*, the central organ of the Eisenach party. p. 45

[41] At the Gotha Congress, the Party's leading organ was composed of representatives of the two organizations. The committee consisted of Wilhelm Hasenclever, Georg Wilhelm Hartmann and Karl de Rossi of the Lassalleans, and August Geib and Ignaz Auer of the Eisenachers. p. 47

[42] In 321 B. C., during the Second Samnite War, the Samnites defeated the Roman army at the Caudine Forks, a defile near the ancient Italian town Caudium and forced the vanquished army to pass under a yoke, a monstrous insult to a defeated army. Hence the term denotes suffering deep humiliation. p. 48

[43] The committee's proposal to remove from the list of Party literature the following works concerning Lassalle: Bernhard Becker, *Revelations About the Tragic Death of Ferdinand Lassalle*, Schleiz, 1868; *The History of Lassalle's Working Class Agitation*, Brunswick, 1874, and Wilhelm Bracke, *The Lassallean Proposal*, Brunswick, 1873. p. 49

[44] The next Reichstag elections were to take place on January 10, 1877. p. 50

[45] Wilhelm Stieber, the head of the Prussian political police. Tessendorf, the public prosecutor in Prussia. p. 50

[46] By the Leipzigers, Engels meant Liebknecht, Bebel and other members of the editorial board of the Party's central organ, *Volksstaat*. p. 50

[47] Kautsky was then editor of the weekly journal *Die Neue Zeit*. p. 54

[48] Victor Adler (1852-1918), the founder and leader of the Austrian Social-Democratic Party. p. 54

[49] Engels' work published not long afterwards under the title, *Brentano Against Marx Because of So-Called Falsified Quotation*, Hamburg, 1891. p. 55

[50] Wilhelm Dietz (1843-1922), a German Social-Democratic member of the Reichstag, was manager of the Party publishing house in Stuttgart, which also put out *Die Neue Zeit.* p. 56

[51] Wilhelm Liebknecht's report on the Party programme on October 15, 1890, at the Halle Congress (see Note 3). p. 56

[52] Eduard Bernstein. p. 58

[53] "Marginal Notes to the Programme of the German Workers' Party" was published in *Die Neue Zeit,* No. 18, January 31, 1891, and in *Vorwärts,* February 1 and 3, 1891.

Vorwärts, the central organ of the German Social-Democratic Party, published in Leipzig, 1876-78, and in Berlin, 1891-1933. Liebknecht and Hasenclever were in charge from 1876 to 1878, and Liebknecht alone from 1891-1900. p. 58

[54] The German Social-Democratic Party leaders attempted to obstruct the distribution of *Die Neue Zeit,* No. 18.

The *Anti-Socialist Law* which outlawed the German Social-Democratic Party was passed by the Bismarck government with majority support in the Reichstag on October 21, 1878, to suppress the socialist and workers' movement. The law was prolonged every 2 to 3 years. As a result of the pressure of the mass workers' movement, the Exceptional Law Against the Socialists was abrogated on October 1, 1890. p. 58

[55] August Bebel. p. 58

[56] *I.e.,* the Eisenachers. p. 59

[57] *Hamburger Echo,* the Social-Democratic daily founded in 1887. p. 61

[58] The editorial "On the Critique of the Social-Democratic Programme, appearing in the *Hamburger Echo,* No. 33, February 8, 1891, indicated the great significance which Engels' publication of Marx's letter on the Gotha Programme had in formulating a new Social-Democratic programme.

Engels here refers to the "system of acquired rights" as expounded by Lassalle in his book of the same title, Leipzig, 1861. Starting from philosophy and jurisprudence, Lassalle interpreted the legal relationships between men from his idealist standpoint. p. 61

[59] A Berlin dispatch in the Vienna *Arbeiter-Zeitung,* No. 6, February 6, 1891, reported that Engels had published in Germany a document of great theoretical and practical significance — Marx's Critique. The author of the dispatch, in commenting on Engels' achievements, wrote further that it was now "time to formulate the theoretical principles of our party

with full sharpness and without any compromise as to the programme, and at the present moment this publication is indeed timely." p. 61

60 Paul Lafargue's article for *Die Neue Zeit*, instead of appearing there as prearranged, was published in *Revue Socialiste*, No. 93, Vol. 16, 1892, under the title "La théorie de la Valeur et de la plus-value de Marx et les économistes bourgeois" ("Marx's Theory of Value and Surplus-Value and the Bourgeois Economists"). p. 62

61 Wilhelm Liebknecht. p. 62

62 Jules Guesde in his "Briefe aus Frankreich" ("Letters from France") which appeared in *Vorwärts*, Nos. 23 and 25, January 28 and 30, 1891, exposed the policy of suppressing the workers' movement at home, which, injurious to the good name of the Republic, was implemented by the moderate bourgeois Republicans — the so-called opportunists — headed by Jean Antoine Ernest Constans, Pierre Maurice Rouvier and others. p. 62

63 On February 13, 1891, in *Vorwärts* was printed an editorial, "Der Marx'sche Programm-Brief" ("Marx's Letter on the Programme"), which expressed the official position of the Party executive on the *Critique of the Gotha Programme.* The article strongly opposed Marx's estimate of Lassalle and his authoritative advice with a "categorical no," and supported the Party's adoption of the draft programme in disregard of Marx's criticism. p. 62

64 August Bebel, Wilhelm Liebknecht and Paul Singer were guests in Engels' home from November 27 to early December 1890 after they went to London on behalf of the German Social-Democratic Party to congratulate Engels on his 70th birthday (November 28, 1890). At Engels' proposal, these representatives of the German Social-Democratic Party met Eleanor Marx-Aveling, John Burns, William Thorne and Cunninghame-Graham, activists in the English working-class movement, to exchange views on problems of the international working-class movement, and in particular, on methods of strengthening the international ties among socialist and workers' parties and organizations. p. 63

65 *Arbeiter-Zeitung*, the central organ of the Austrian Social-Democratic Party, founded by Victor Adler in 1889 in Vienna. p. 65

66 This letter was first published in *Internationale Presse Korrespondenz*, Berlin, Vol. XII, No. 11, February 9, 1932. p. 67

67 The reference is to *Critique of the Gotha Programme.* p. 67

68 *Sächsische Arbeiter-Zeitung*, the Social-Democratic Party paper published in Dresden from 1890.

Züricher Post, a Swiss Social-Democratic paper, published from December 1890 to April 1891. p. 68

[69] *Die Neue Zeit* carried the *Vorwärts* editorial, No. 37, February 13, 1891 (see Note 63), in Vol. I, No. 21, 1890-91. Besides its introduction to the *Vorwärts* editorial, the *Neue Zeit* editorial board stated: "The fact is, we don't feel duty bound to submit this letter by Marx to the leadership and/or fraction of the Social-Democratic Party for their consideration. We alone bear the responsibility for publishing it." p. 68

[70] As a lawyer, Lassalle handled the divorce case of Countess Sophie Hatzfeldt from 1845 to 1854. p. 69

[71] Johann Baptist von Schweitzer (1833-75), the leader of the Lassalleans after Lassalle's death. p. 70

[72] Engels was preparing the fourth edition of *The Origin of the Family, Private Property and the State*, 1891. p. 71

[73] Richard Fischer (1855-1926), a member of the German Social-Democratic Party executive and the manager of the Berlin Party publishing house.

In his letter of February 20, 1891, Richard Fischer notified Engels of the Party executive's decision to re-publish Marx's *The Civil War in France* and *Wage-Labour and Capital* and Engels' *Socialism: Utopian and Scientific*, and asked him to write prefaces for the new editions. p. 71

[74] *New-Yorker Volkszeitung*, founded by and under the direction of Frederick Sorge in 1878. p. 72

[75] In a letter of March 30, 1891, August Bebel gave his reasons for remaining silent for so long. He was unwilling to give a direct answer after the publication of Marx's letter on the programme because he disagreed with the way it was done; besides, he was involved in Reichstag activities. Bebel considered it improper to publish Marx's covering letter to Bracke, May 5, 1875, for, he claimed, it concerned not the Party programme but the Party leadership. He gave as his main reason for opposing its publication that it placed weapons in the hands of the enemy to fight the socialists, while the sharp criticism of Lassalle would irritate the ex-Lassalleans in the Party.

In his letter of April 25, 1891, Bebel gave Engels an account of the German workers' movement and mentioned in particular the strike of the Rhine-Westphalian coal miners. He considered the strike untimely, as it would be favourable to the mine-owners who had been seeking excuses to smother the miners' discontent. In the face of the probability of police provocation particularly on the eve of May Day, the Party executive warned the miners not to take premature action. p. 74

[76] Audorf's prologue was written for the commemoration on September 4, 1876, of the anniversary of Ferdinand Lassalle's death. p. 78

[77] *Der Vorbote* (*Herald*), a German anarchist paper published in Chicago from 1881. p. 78

马 克 思
哥达纲领批判
*
外文出版社出版（北京）
1972年（32开）第一版
编号：（英）1050—2083
00039
1/1—E—1190P